VERSES IN PEACE AND WAR

BY
SHANE LESLIE

LONDON
Burns and Oates Ltd.
28 Orchard Street
1916

NOTE.—Some of these verses, which have already appeared separately in *Eyes of Youth*, *The Armagh Hymnal*, *The Leader*, *The Irish Homestead*, *The Tablet*, *The Westminster Gazette*, and *The Cambridge Review*, are setting sail for a second time to the shores of oblivion—and in suitable company.

Printed in England

In the interest of creating a more extensive selection of rare historical book reprints, we have chosen to reproduce this title even though it may possibly have occasional imperfections such as missing and blurred pages, missing text, poor pictures, markings, dark backgrounds and other reproduction issues beyond our control. Because this work is culturally important, we have made it available as a part of our commitment to protecting, preserving and promoting the world's literature. Thank you for your understanding.

CONTENTS

TRANSCENDENTAL : P. 7.
BALLAD OF TWO SISTERS : P. 7.
LOVE AND DEATH : P. 8.
THE WISH : P. 9.
PLEDGE : P. 10.
THE MOUNTAIN AND THE SEA : P. 10.
RUBIES : P. 11.
THE TWO MOTHERS : P. 11.
THE CENTENARIAN : P. 12.
A BALLAD OF CHINA TEA : P. 12.
BOG LOVE : P. 13.
MI-CARÊME IN CONNAUGHT : P. 14.
HOLY LAND : P. 15.
LORD OF THE SOUL : P. 15.
SECONDS : P. 16.
SISTER SHADOW : P. 17.
SYMBOLISM : P. 17.
SAINT JOHN BAPTIST : P. 18.
TRISTE LIGNUM : P. 18.
THE JUDGMENT OF PILATE : P. 19.
HOLY CROSS : P. 19.
THE GREAT MEMORY : P. 21.
THE TRINITY : P. 21.
SATAN : P. 22.
NIGHTMARE : P. 22.
THE BEE : P. 23.

THE DEAD FRIEND : P. 23.
MASS FOR THE DEAD : P. 24.
THE PHILOSOPHY OF PAIN : P. 25.
TO TOLSTOI DYING : P. 25.
EPITAPHS FOR AVIATORS—
    ROLLS : P. 25.
    CHAVEZ : P. 25.
    HAMEL : P. 26.
    WARNEFORD, V.C. : P. 26.
    LIDDELL, V.C. : P. 26.
EPITAPHS FOR SOLDIERS—
    AFTER MONS : P. 26.
    HIGHLANDER : P. 27.
    THE MUNSTERS : P. 27.
    THE WINEPRESS : P. 27.
    THE SENTRY : P. 27.
IN PIAM MEMORIAM—
    MIDSHIPMAN ALLSOPP : P. 28.
    LIEUT. CHARLES LISTER : P. 28.
    LIEUT. RUPERT BROOKE : P. 28.
    CAPTAIN NORMAN LESLIE : P. 28.
AS AT THERMOPYLÆ : P. 29.
THE HURDLERS : P. 29.
THE RACERS : P. 30.
SPRING 1915 : P. 30.

VERSES IN PEACE AND WAR

TRANSCENDENTAL

If my soul gat your glory for raiment
   And donned your bright beauty for dress,
If he won for all misery's payment
   The robes of your loveliness.

Then the sunshine of earth would seem shade,
   And dim would the starlight be,
Nor would Solomon seem so arrayed
   With such softness and splendour as he!

BALLAD OF TWO SISTERS

The little Sister's Sister is the writer's wife
(For ANNE and MARJORIE IDE)

My Sister, oh my little Sister
   Down from Heaven came to play,
And the mighty angels missed her
   More than song or sigh could say.

My Sister, oh my little Sister
   God made of sun and star and clay,
But she might have been His Sister
   For the Love that in her lay.

My Sister for another Sister
   Unto God did sweetly pray,
Till He made a second Sister
   In His grand Almighty way.

And my Sister's little Sister,
   A second bud upon the spray
Left the Angels like her Sister
   Wondering what to sigh or say.

So my Sister's little Sister
   Came to help her with her play,
Whom God made as like her Sister
   As the light is like the day.

My Sister and her little Sister
   Are to each as June to May,
For June and May are ever Sister,
   And none so sweet or fair as they.

Envoi

But God forgive me if I kissed her,
   For it was the only way
To tell my Sister's little Sister
   What the Angels could not say!

LOVE AND DEATH

Of the twain of the Gods who reign greatest
   Of all the Lords gracious above,
The Giver of Good who gives latest—
   Death—spoke in his jesting to Love:

"Dear boy, are mine arrows not stronger
  Than any of thine are made strong?
Though lighter, they linger the longer
  Whomever they lighten among.

"For those whom thou woundest but sicken
  And seldom drop ravished of breath—
But surely and strait are they stricken
  By wounding from me who am Death."

Him answered Love smiling: "O reaver
  Of Life, is thy wounding so sore?
Though my lovers but languish in fever
  Thy dead love a thousand times more!"

THE WISH [1]

THERE is one moment each day
  If only we knew,
When the wish we dared to say
  Would surely come true.

I've watched the coming of dawn
  —My wish in my mouth!—
I've watched till the mists up-drawn
  Blew into the South.

I've watched each hour of Noon
  —My wish on my tongue!—
Till skies went weird with the Moon
  And hearth-crickets sung.

[1] An Irish belief that *once* in twenty-four hours a wish is fulfilled—if uttered at the exact second.

But the wish I wished all day
  Would never come true,
For the wish I dared not say
  With my lips—was *you*!

PLEDGE

Thou art my Sister, Mother, Wife—
  In God's own likeness One and Three.
Thou givest light and love and life,
  I give my soul's full faith to thee.

THE MOUNTAIN AND THE SEA

Said the Mountain to the Sea:
"I am laden loving thee,
And my tears of melted snow
Bring you token down below."
To the Mountain sang the Sea:
"All my tideways throb for thee.
Winter night and Summer day
Clamber I to creek and bay."
Circled by the lonely lea
Yearned the Mountain for the Sea,
While across the barren sand
Strove the Sea to come to Land.
Godlike Mountain, Virgin Sea—
Never shall they mingled be
Till the waves are foam and gust,
Till the hill-tops die to dust.

When the years are come and done,
When all love is lost or won—
Then the winds shall set them free,
Ash of Mountain—Mist of Sea!

RUBIES

The fickle rubies sleeping in your hair
The ladies of another age shall wear,
But here are living drops in every vein
That no one's love shall e'er make red again!

THE TWO MOTHERS

On the hill of weeping
Mother Mary spake unto Granuaile:[1]
"Little Mother, why so sad and pale?"
"Half my sons are sleeping,"
Unto Mother Mary said Granuaile,
"And the rest are keeping
Weary watch beneath a windless sail."
"Mother, hush your weeping,"
Mary Mother said unto Granuaile:
"They are in my keeping
Where their hearts and hands can never fail,
And the rest are sleeping
But to rise again in freedom's gale,"
Mary Mother spake unto Granuaile.

[1] Granuaile—an Irish Sea-Queen whose name is symbolic for Ireland herself.

THE CENTENARIAN

"All the hundred of years
I have lived on the road by the hill,
All the turf in the world would not fill
My unresting wee hearthful of flame,
But the passing of folk went the same
　All that hundred of years—
For they tramped up the hill and the road
Till the day they were drawn like a load,
Yet the fire of the world is not fed
Though I'm watching the dead join the dead
　For a hundred of years."

A BALLAD OF CHINA TEA

When the windboy is out on the eaves
　And blowing the rain from his lip,
Then I boil me the brown fairy leaves
　That crossed the Red Sea in a ship.

Oh, the music they pipe in their brewing
　Makes many thoughts dance in mine eye,
And the breath of the wise water stewing—
　It curls to my heart with a sigh.

As I think of old friends, and of all
　Who will never turn homeward again,
And the children I'm longing to call
　From where they lie out in the rain.

Oh, the dark steaming dew I let soak
   On my weary old brain, till the floor
Is laden with feet and the folk
   In Americay come to the door.

Oh, hours they do sit with me drinking,
   While the jealous wind sings on the pane,
Oh, hours we sit lonesome and thinking
   On friends who are out in the rain.

And when drinking has left the leaves dry
   As the tide leaves the sea-weary cress,
Then a wee shadow starts with a cry
   And clutches the hem of my dress.

And I rise myself up to the wall,
   And weep out a heartful of pain—
For it's little dead children that call
   Their old mother in out of the rain.

BOG LOVE

Wee Shemus was a misdropt man
   Without a shoulder to his back;
He had the way to lift a rann
   And throttled rabbits in a sack.

And red-haired Mary, whom he wed,
   Brought him but thirty shillings told;
She had but one eye in her head,
   But Shemus counted it for gold.

The two went singing in the hay
   Or kissing underneath the sloes,
And where they chanced to pass the day
   There was no need to scare the crows.

But now with Mary waked and laid
   As decent as she lived and died,
Poor Shemus went to buy a spade
   To dig himself a place beside.

MÌ CARÊME IN CONNAUGHT

THE Bishop is up at the Synod,
   The priest is gone riding away—
So we'll quit from our fasting and weeping
   And give ourselves up to our play.

Too long we are living on praties
   And sea-smelly fish from the bay;
We'll boil up a sliver of bacon
   And butter our bread for the day.

For it's hard to be always out feeding
   On turnips and gruel and hay—
So here is dead meat in a splutter
   And a smell of white milk in the tay!

But God in His Pity forgive us
   If we ate for a while this day,
For the Bishop is gone to the Synod
   And the Curate is out on his grey.

HOLY LAND

Oh, had the Lord once chosen thee, O Ireland,
  And led thy dreaming Druids with a Star,
Oh, had He chosen thee to be His Sireland,
  Thy Hills would not be holier than they are.

Not holier—had in Irish been the prayer
  Of her to whom Saint Gabriel was sent,
And had Saint Joseph trudged to Galway fair
  To pay the middleman his bit of rent.

Nor dearer would I love thee, had He spoken
  To tell of coming sorrow unto thee,
And walked thy lanes and stood, oh splendid token !
  Upon the Shannon as she strikes the sea.

And had He blessed the poor and weak, O Mother,
  Standing on some green mountain top of thine
And breathed his life away upon another,
  To me thou wert not holier, Land of mine.

LORD OF THE SOUL

As one who hears his wife from sleep call clear
  Upon some former lover's name,
And rends his heart in agonies of fear
  Lest *he* should come again—who came—
And like a thief pass unseen through the night
  By ways about the heart once trod,
So Satan trembles when some sinful wight
  Cries out unwittingly to God !

SECONDS

One by one, the silent-sounding seconds come,
Making music in their millions—yet so dumb—

Hundreds pass like one, tho' each hath separate been,
One with Time, tho' Time itself lies each between.

By their coming, in their wake the lives of men are shed;
Men with them are born and in their dying dead.

One by one they march with noiseless thunder shod,
Treading out the living as the dead were trod.

No one second lingers long or seemeth soon,
Each comes stripped of sorrow, each goes bared of boon.

For no single second here can compass peace,
Nor a thousand make sweet Hope's last hoping cease—

Though they tramp the Stars to dust and bleed the Sun,
Ere they have finished coming, going one by one!

SISTER SHADOW

Sister Shadow, dost thou watch me all the way?
Comrade of my cares and phantom of my play—
Now I see thee in the sunshine dancing near,
Closer clinging than a lover, Shadow dear.

But when days of storm and darkness cover me,
Thou dost closer creep than human eye can see,
Sister Shadow, when I cross the Bridge of Death,
Wilt thou longer stay with me than Brother
    Breath?

Him I see in winter, thee in summertide—
But there comes a winter when he leaves my side;
Sister Shadow, may I hold thee by the hand
When I come at lonely last to Shadowland?

SYMBOLISM

Our garden wall: the fruit-trees that we know,
    The Sundial turning every way—
Recall the piteous moment long ago
    Man lost his Paradisal day.

The daylight's columned clouds: the rays that
    glow
    From every golden sunset's pyre
Mask and reveal the God who long ago
    Went by in guise of smoke or fire.

His Hands, His Feet seem fast to every bough!
  His Blood drips under every hedge!
Who took the thorn and timber long ago
  To be our long-lost Eden's pledge.

SAINT JOHN BAPTIST

O Herod, cowering 'neath a woman's deed,
Not as you thought a bending reed—
Behold the Baptist strong to bleed!

Alone he kept his desert tryst,
For dancing feet his head was priced—
Slain is the Shadow of the Christ.

Thou canst not quell the prophet's breath.
"Prepare the way of God"—he saith,
"Make straight His paths before, O Death."

The dead shall hear his lonely cry,
"Lo, comes a mightier One than I,
The Lord of Life and Death is nigh!"

TRISTE LIGNUM

When Christ said to the barren tree,
"For lacking fruit accursèd be"—
The withered bough replied: "O God,
Didst Thou but set me in the sod

To mar me of my juicy seed,
Whereon might passing pilgrims feed?"
Whom answered Christ with sudden grief:
"Thou shalt then have My life for leaf,
And men shall fasten fruit on thee
When they are crucifying Me."

THE JUDGMENT OF PILATE

When the soul of Pilate fled below
Nigh on nineteen hundred years ago—
He was asked: "Dost thou remember Him,
Thou didst kill to please a rabble's whim?"

"Out of all I judged by Roman code,
Taking life or limb for what they owed;
I remember once I bade the Jews
One from two compatriots choose—
There was thief Barabbas whom they won.
But I have forgot the Other One—
Who He was or whence, or what He said."

Answered then the Judge of quick and dead:
"Pilate, this thy only doom shall be,
Not to know for all eternity!"

HOLY CROSS

It is the bare and leafless Tree
Our sins once sowed on Calvary,
And mockers digged with trembling knee.

It is the dead unpitying Wood,
That like a crimson pillar stood,
Where none unmoved, unweeping could—

O fearful sight foretold to man,
The cloven spar, the sacred span
Whence God's atoning Blood once ran.

It is the Holy Gibbet Tree,
All stained with Love's last agony
And marked with awful mystery.

What stains are these incarnadine?
What scars are these more red than Wine
Of more than human Passion sign?

What storms swept on its boughs that day,
When God to God did sorely pray,
And human guilt ebbed slow away!

It is the sunless stricken Tree
Upon whose branches sore to see,
O mystery! died One of Three.

When earth shall smoke and sun shall flee,
Alone, unmoved on sinking sea
Shall stand one all-redeeming Tree.

THE GREAT MEMORY

As visions start from dreams forgot as soon as
    dreamt,
  O God, does e'er the Lake of Galilee
With little ships and hills and fishermen unkempt
  Rise out of Thine Eternity to Thee?

THE TRINITY

They sit with doom upon their knees
Who made the world, the skies and seas,
O mystery of mysteries—
              The Trinity!
O Father, birthless, deathless One,
Whose Beauty we have gazed upon
And seen the Sole-Begotten Son—
              In Trinity!
O Christ, Whom pain supremely trod
In agonies that shook the sod,
Yet wast ungrieved, unpassioned God—
              The Trinity!
O Spirit, brooding o'er the deep
Who givest us of life to weep—
But yet art winged with death and sleep—
              In Trinity!
Pervading whence all space must flee,
Where numbers fail, accounted Three,
Where nothing is, shall ever be—
              The Trinity!

SATAN

He stood beside me suddenly,
More bright than Sun or Cloud to see,
A gentle beauty bathing him—
'Twas godlike Satan, soul and limb!

His hair was white as burning snow.
His eyes retained the quiet glow
Of courtesies in holier time,
His lips let forth a silver chime.

Then at each lustrous sign he bore,
I would have knelt me to adore—
When Someone cried that clutched my dress:
" Rise up—he loves his loveliness! "

NIGHTMARE

I dreamt that the Heavens were beggared
    And Angels went chanting for bread,
That the Cherubs were sewed up in sackcloth
    And Satan anointed his head!

I dreamt they had chalked up a price
    On the Sun and the Stars at God's feet,
And the Devil had bought up the Church
    And put out the Pope in the street!

THE BEE

"Away," the old monks said,
　"Sweet honey-fly,
From lilting overhead
　The lullaby
You heard some mother croon
Beneath the harvest moon.
Go, hum it in the Hive,"
　The old monks said—
"For we were once alive
　Who now are dead."

THE DEAD FRIEND

In Memoriam: Joseph Stickney of Harvard, U.S.A.

I DREW him then unto my knees,
　My friend who was dead,
And I set my live lips over his,
　And my heart to his head.

I thought of an unrippled love
　And a passion unsaid,
All the years he was living by me—
　My friend who was dead.

And the white morning ways that we went,
　And how oft we had fed
And drunk with the sunset for lamp
　—Myself and the dead.

Then I spake unto God in my grief:
  "My wine and my bread,
And my staff, Thou hast taken from me
  —My friend who is dead.

"Are the Heavens yet friendless to Thee,
  And lone to Thy Head,
That Thy desolate Heart hath need
  Of my friend who is dead?"

To God then I spake yet again:
  "Not Peter instead
Would I take, nor Philip nor John
  For my friend who is dead."

MASS FOR THE DEAD

In Memoriam: John Stratford Collins

O GOD, and hast Thou slain my love?
  And are Thy Feet and Hands not red?
O Eagle, hast Thou snatched a dove
  Away to Heaven's Eyrie dead?

But Thou hast suffered for his sake—
  "This is My Body"—Thou hast said,
And mourning priests Thy flesh shall break
  And Blood of Thine for his be shed!

THE PHILOSOPHY OF PAIN

Supposing Pain herself were stricken dead,
  And Time crept on without annoy,
Then Life would lack the salt upon his bread
  And Joy would haply die of Joy.

TO TOLSTOI DYING

Gaunt soul of goaded Russia agonising,
  How grandly thou hast failed to keep thy tryst.
Of all mankind till now we hail thee noblest rising
  —But there has been no Christian since the Christ!

EPITAPHS FOR AVIATORS

ROLLS

Leap high, ye coursers of the wind,
  Against this Church's steadfast aisle—
It guardeth one of mortal kind,
  Who bridled you a little while.

CHAVEZ

One flying past the Alps to see
  What lay beyond their crest—
Behind the snows found Italy
  Beyond the mountains—rest.

HAMEL

Nor rugged earth nor untamed sky
Gave him his death to die,
But gentlest of the Holy Three—
The long grey liquid Sea.

LIEUT. WARNEFORD, V.C.

Say not his life is little worth
  Whose broken wings are made his shroud;
Death men have met on sea and earth,
  But he hath slain him in the cloud.

CAPT. AIDAN LIDDELL, V.C.

Another one of mortal birth
  Hath set his spirit free.
Lie very lightly on him, Earth,
  Who did not tread on thee.

EPITAPHS FOR SOLDIERS

AFTER MONS

We lie like castaways upon the shore
  Whose lives were lost upon the Great Retreat,
But whither ebb hath been, the flow shall pour,
  And we await the tide's returning feet.

HIGHLANDER

He sleeps with claymore in his tartan furled—
    The mud of Flanders stains his knee.
Farewell, O hills and far-off Gaelic world!
    Farewell, sweet Hebridean Sea!

THE MUNSTERS

By long, long ways they'll travel home again,
    The few of us who are not stricken down,
But we, who yestereve in fight were slain,
    This day shall be in Tipperary Town!

THE WINEPRESS

O Englishmen unborn, whene'er your tongue
    Is sweet with wines from Frankish sod,
Remember that its joyous juice was wrung
    From fields your kindred deathward trod.

THE SENTRY

"Who passeth here?"—"We of the new Brigade,
    Who come in aid—to take your place who fell."
"What is the countersign?"—"That we have weighed
    The cost ye paid—yet come!"—"Pass! all is well."

IN PIAM MEMORIAM

MIDSHIPMAN ALLSOPP—CHILE

No earth to earth need fall on darkening grave
 For one who dies away at sea—
Nor tears mingle with the radiant wave,
 That guards his boyish purity.

LIEUT. CHARLES LISTER—GALLIPOLI

"At home, in youth's hot flush—friend of the folk
 I was, and spokesman of their plight,
Who now far off, beneath a warrior's cloak,
 Lie slain for every people's right."

LIEUT. RUPERT BROOKE—LEMNOS

Thou wert to England's living Helicon
 A star of dawn as bright as swiftly shed—
And now at sudden eve—with life undone—
 Thy loveliness is light unto the dead!

CAPTAIN NORMAN LESLIE—ARMENTIÈRES

What though he lies far from his rainbow isle
 Of greenlit trees and holy lake;
He doth but sleep awhile, the little while
 Till those, who cannot die, awake!

AS AT THERMOPYLÆ

S*tranger*, since we could but die—
 If the English have not heard,
Tell them that their soldiers lie
 Here, obedient to their word.

THE HURDLERS[1]

In Memoriam: Gerald Anderson, Kenneth Powell

Oh, how are the beautiful broken,
 And how are the swiftest made slow—
What pity, what praise may be spoken
 When England's Olympians lie low?

Like greyhounds, they tore from their tether,
 And loosened life's leash on their soul,
And now that they perish together—
 Not last have they come to the goal.

They were slain in the great endeavour
 To stem the barbarian Day,
But the deed of their dying shall never
 Pass voiceless or vainly away.

From home and from far-away regions,
 From trading and township and shire
Rise 'Varsity men in their legions
 To hand on the torch of their fire.

[1] Hurdlers for England at the last Olympian games.

Yet dead are the champions we cherished,
  And fallen, alas, not in play—
Oh, how have the beautiful perished,
  The swiftest passed swiftest away!

THE RACERS

A PROPHET through his magic periscope
Peered through the distant, deeply rushing ways—
Across Time's dim partitioning to days
Whereon each nation stakes her shuddering hope,
And saw huge horses pass across the haze,
Whose riders gave them neither spur nor praise,
But let them charge unheld by rein or rope.
The first was Red: his Rider held a Sword,
Which wounded Peace and cut her silver Cord.
The second one was Black, with Death for Prong.
The third was Pale: Death was his Stable-Lord,
And far as eye could reach, a wretched throng
Of dying men cried out: "O God, how long?"

SPRING 1915

MARCHING to-day we heard the first thrush sing
  To prophesy of seasons four.
Ah well-a-day for those to whom the Spring
  Shall spring remain for evermore!

CPSIA information can be obtained at www.ICGtesting.com
Printed in the USA
LVOW090034260613

340231LV00007B/36/P